Fall 1981   Volume IV Number 3

Paperback Quarterly

"Journal of
Mass-Market Paperback History"

Contents

Paperback Quarterly Publications
Brownwood, Texas

Paperback Quarterly specializes in the history of mass market paperbacks. Its goal is to make the study of paperback history more comprehensive and reliable.

Paperback Quarterly features articles and notes dealing with every type (mystery, detective, science fiction, western, adventure, etc) and with every aspect of new, old and rare paperbacks.

Emphasis is placed on the historical research of paperbacks, their authors, illustrators, publishers and distributors, but the editors also invite contributions of bibliographical interest. In short, the only criterion for the editors' consideration is that the subject matter pertain to paperbacks.

Paperback Quarterly pays 1¢ per word (200-2000 words) for articles and notes. Payment also includes two copies of the issue in which your article appears.

Paperback Quarterly is published in Spring, Summer, Fall and Winter of each year with a subscription rate of $10.00 per year or individual copies for $3.50 each. Institutional and library subscriptions are $12.00 per year. Overseas rate is $15.00. All back issues are out of print.

All correspondence, articles, notes, queries, ads and subscriptions should be sent to 1710 Vincent St., Brownwood, Texas 76801. (915) 643-1182.

Ad rate card on request.

Published and Edited by

Charlotte Laughlin   Billy C. Lee

Contributing Editors

Bill Crider   Michael S. Barson
William Lyles   Thomas L. Bonn

Printer and Technical Advisor
Martin E. Gottschalk

Copy Editor
Judy Crider

Cover logo designed by Peter Manesis

Norman Daniels
the Writer as Assemblyline
by Michael Barson

The career of Norman Daniels parallels that
of Harry Whittington (see PQ IV/2) in many ways.
Like Whittington, he was on the scene when
paperback originals first emerged in 1950, and
sold dozens of novels under a variety of pseudonyms to the digest lines in just a few years.
Like Whittington, he went on to do numerous
adaptations from films and television shows,
along with the briefly popular Nurse romances
during the Sixties. And, like Whittington, he
ended up the Seventies by authoring (along with
his wife, Dorothy) a series of Southern Historicals, or Plantation Sagas, which plug into the
current trend in mass market fiction. But while
their versatility overlaps, Daniels and Whittington have had careers which bear their own dis-
tinctive stamps.

A star of the pulp magazines since the mid-
Thirties, when his byline appeared in SPICY DE-
TECTIVE and DIME DETECTIVE, Norman Daniels had
already had hundreds of stories published by
1950 when the paperback houses began looking for
original manuscripts. Moreover, he had authored
scores of NICK CARTER radio shows during the
late Forties. Thus, when the paperback market
opened up, Daniels recognized it as simply the
next phase of popular entertainment, and set
about the business of selling to it.

Reading his digest novels, one recognizes
that Daniels did not exert himself overmuch in
writing them. And why should he have? The pay-
day for a potboiler like SHACK GIRL or MISTRESS
ON A DEATH BED would always be the same paltry
$500 to $800, even if the manuscript one turned
in was another WAR AND PEACE. And how good
could one make an adaptation of "Ben Casey" or
"The Rat Patrol"? No one knows how good a

writer Norman Daniels really was, or is, because he has never tried to create a work of
art or make a personal statement in his work.
Instead, the dozens of gothics he co-authored
with Dorothy, the mysteries, the westerns, the
nurse stories all were treated equally, as work
that was done for a paycheck. One wonders
what might have been had those hundreds of
pieces of work not been just assembled, like so
many transmissions. But then, the world needs
transmissions, too.

Norman Daniels has always been successful
at what he has tried to do; his list of publishing credits speaks for itself. But Daniels
will never be "discovered" by fans of paperback
fiction, as recently Jim Thompson and Harry
Whittington have been discovered, because the
passionless quality of his writing insures a
like response from his readers. And if all of
Daniels' work crumbles into dust, as it seems
fated to do, the man will have no complaint,
any more than a bricklayer can be sorry when
his garage finally falls into disrepair. A
garage isn't the Sistine chapel, and the works
of Norman Daniels will never be mistaken for
art. That's the razor's edge for the pro-
fessional writer of paperbacks, who accepts the
commonly perceived mediocrity of the medium and
never tries to pull it up by its bootstraps.

But keep this in mind: without writers
like Norman Daniels, there would not be any
paperback industry. Every industry needs
products. Daniels supplies them. Here we
have commerce. And in Daniels, a laborer
worthy of his hire.

An Interview with Norman Daniels
by Michael S. Barson

MB: In the early 1950s you used the pen names
      of David Wade, Mark Reed, Norma Dann and
      James Clayford for such paperback digest
      houses as Falcon and Rainbow books. Could
      you describe the operations at these houses,
      and why they eventually folded?

ND: Falcon and other small houses were mainly
      fly-by-night types. They offered no edi-
      torial guidelines; they paid about half of
      what the larger houses did. They wanted
      only stories which were, at that time,
      considered "hot"--by today's standards they
      could have been read in Bible class. At
      that time there was a concentrated effort
      to rid the stands of "dirty" books; Falcon
      and the others sent out their books and the
      newsdealers were afraid to unpack them.
      Pen names were used because these books were,
      in plain English, garbage. I did not enjoy
      writing these things, but at the time the
      better companies were in a doldrum and not
      buying.

MB: Before cracking the paperback originals
      market, you wrote thousands of stories for
      the pulps. Did you find the transition
      from one market to another difficult?

ND: Writing for the pulps was radically differ-
      ent from books. Nothing was the same--
      plotting, quality of writing, time spent,
      etc. For me, the transition was easy.

MB: Another of your successes lay in the medium
      of radio. Did you ever return to those
      hundreds of "Nick Carter" scripts for story

5

ideas? How did writing for radio compare to writing for the paperback market?

ND: I never used a radio plot for a fiction story. Radio was the easiest form of writing I have ever done. It paid fairly well in those days. I also have a number of TV shows to my credit--Hitchcock, G. E. Theatre, etc. This was, and is, the worst form of writing in history.

MB: Authors such as Michael Avallone, John Jakes and Harry Whittington have complained about the lack of royalties they received for their novelizations of popular TV shows. What have your experiences been in this area?

ND: Long ago I wrote Dr. Kildare, Ben Casey and some others. The advances were fair for those days, but I'm sure I never received a royalty. It was impossible to make any money on these.

MB: Among the genres you've worked in are gothics, romances, westerns, mysteries, spy novels, suspense and plantation novels. Is there one you prefer over the others?

ND: For types, the gothics were fun to do. Historicals were also profitable, as were the plantations. I'm currently working on a series for Warner--three 200,000 worders are already in print--that deals with slavery before, during and after the Civil War. This is the "Wynward" series, and it's doing very well.

MB: It seems to me that the symbiotic relation- ship you and Mrs. Daniels have in writing gothics is amazing--some you write, some she writes, and some are collaborations.

6

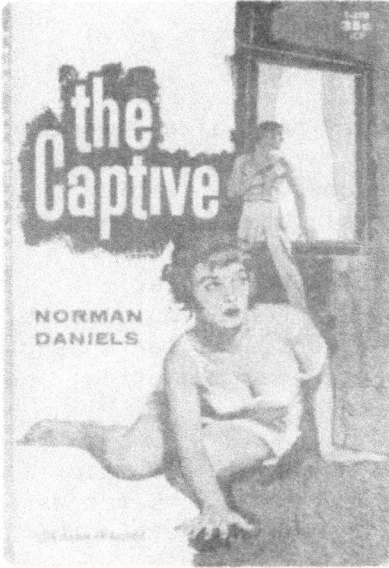

Paperbacks by Norman Daniels

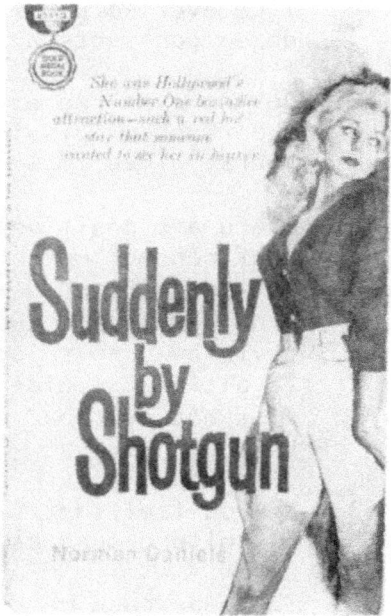

Paperbacks by Norman Daniels

Can you tell by reading the work years
after the fact who wrote what?

ND: My wife, Dorothy, and I have always worked
     together. Sometimes I write the first
     draft; sometimes she does. In reading over
     old books, we can't tell who wrote what.

MB: You have had work published by nearly a
     dozen paperback houses. Could you discuss
     the ways in which the houses differ in such
     areas as editorial guidance, promotion, and
     pay scales?

ND: The paperback houses do not differ materially.
     At this point I do most of my work for Warner
     Books. I have more or less free rein there
     and I work directly under the editor-in-
     chief. Warner does good promotion, pays
     very well, and is the most reliable outfit
     I've ever worked for. Warner has us a half-
     dozen contracts ahead.

MB: Do you ever regret having produced primarily
     paperback originals over the last thirty
     years, given their lesser status by critics?

ND: There are positively no regrets for having
     confined our work to paperbacks. We have,
     in fact, turned down a number of offers
     from hardcover. Paperbacks are fun: no
     revisions, no rejections, fast pay, good
     royalties. Incidentally, neither I nor my
     wife has ever had a book rejected. We keep
     busy.

MB: Do you feel that the paperback industry is
     on solid ground as it moves into the 1980s?

ND: The paperback market is healthier than ever
     and, in my opinion, is overtaking the hard-
     cover outfits. However, I do not like the

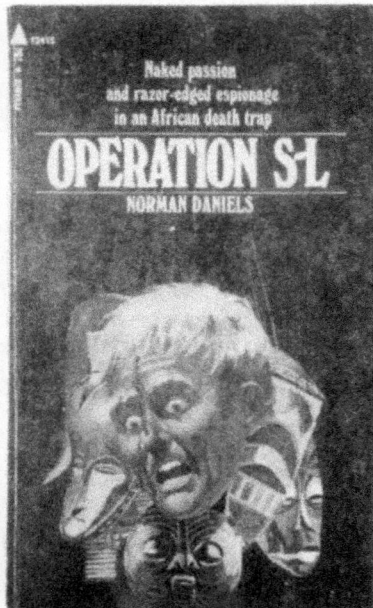

Paperbacks by Norman Daniels

conglomerates taking over everything they can buy. I believe the quality cf books will not hold up as well as if the houses were run individually, as they used to be.

A Chronology of Paperback Originals by Norman Daniels

WANTON BY NIGHT. Ecstasy Novel #15, 1951. As James Clayford.

COME NIGHT, COME DESIRE. Ecstasy Novel #17, 1951. As David Wade.

GIVE ME ECSTASY. Exotic Novel #18, 1951. As Mark Reed.

FOUR DAMES NAMED SIN. Rainbow #105, 1951. As Mark Reed.

STREET OF DARK DESIRES. Rainbow Book #107, 1951. As Mark Reed.

WALK THE EVIL STREET. Rainbow Book #111, 1952. As David Wade.

SHE WALKS BY NIGHT. Rainbow Book #116, 1952. As David Wade.

BEDROOM IN HELL. Rainbow Book #117, 1952.

TEASE THE WILD FLAME. Rainbow Book #114, 1952. As Mark Reed.

THE NUDE STRANGER. Rainbow Book #120, 1952. As Mark Reed.

THE SCARLET BRIDE. Falcon Book #22, 1952. As Mark Reed.

LAY DOWN AND DIE. Falcon Book #26, 1952. As Mark Reed.

LIDA LYNN. Falcon Book #27, 1952. As Norma Dann.

MISTRESS ON A DEATH BED. Falcon Mystery #29, 1952.

VICE COP. Rainbow Book #123, 1952. As Mark Reed.

BEDROOM WITH A VIEW. Rainbow Book #124, 1952. As David Wade.

SINS OF THE FLESH. Falcon Book #32, 1952. As Mark Reed.

SHACK GIRL. Falcon Book #34, 1952. As Norma Dann.

RAISE THE DEVIL. Falcon Book #35, 1952. As
    David Wade.
SWEET SAVAGE. Falcon Book #38, 1952.
THE TWIST. Rainbow Book #128, 1953. As Norma
    Dann.
ONLY HUMAN. Rainbow Book #129, 1953. As David
    Wade.
HOUSE OF A THOUSAND DESIRES. Falcon Book #43,
    1953. As Mark Reed.
THE DEADLY GAME. Avon #864, 1959.
THE CAPTIVE. Avon T-370, 1959.
LADY FOR SALE. Avon #868, 1960.
SINNERS WILD. Avon #874, 1960. As Mark Reed.
SOME DIE RUNNING. Avon #876, 1960.
LOVER LET ME LIVE. Avon T-479, 1960.
SPY HUNT. Pyramid G571, 1960.
SUDDENLY BY SHOTGUN. Gold Medal, 1961.
SHADOW OF A DOUBT. Gold Medal, 1961. As
    Harrison Judd.
JENNIFER JAMES, R. N. Gold Medal, 1961.
BEN CASEY: A RAGE FOR JUSTICE. Lancer, 1962.
    Based on television series.
COUNTY HOSPITAL. Gold Medal, 1963.
SOMETHING BURNING. Gold Medal, 1963.
ARREST AND TRIAL. Lancer, 1963. Based on
    television series.
THE MISSING WITNESS. Lancer, 1964. Based on
    "Arrest and Trial" television series.
THE HUNT CLUB. Pyramid, 1964.
BATTALION. Pyramid, 1965.
OVERKILL. Pyramid, 1964.
SPY GHOST. Pyramid, 1965.
THE UNGUARDED. Lancer 1965. As Dorothy Daniels.
MOMENTS OF GLORY. Paperback Library, 1965.
OPERATION K. Pyramid, 1965. THE MAN FROM A.P.E.
    series.
OPERATION N. Pyramid, 1965. THE MAN FROM A.P.E.
    series.
THE RAT PATROL. Paperback Library, 1966. Based
    on television series.
NURSE AT DANGER MANSION. Lancer 1966. As
    Dorothy Daniels.

Paperbacks by Norman Daniels

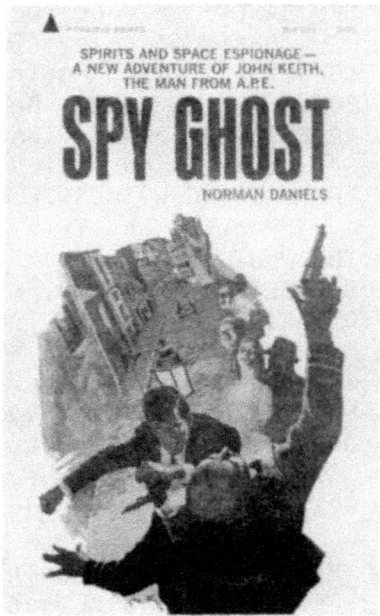

Paperbacks by Norman Daniels

OPERATION T. Pyramid, 1967. THE MAN FROM A.P.E.
    series.
OPERATION VC. Pyramid, 1967. THE MAN FROM
    A.P.E. series.
THE FORBIDDEN CITY. Berkley, 1967. MAYA #1.
    Based on television series.
THE BARON OF HONG KONG. Lancer, 1967.
BARON'S MISSION TO PEKING. Lancer, 1968.
THE TARNISHED SCALPEL. Lancer, 1968.
THE MAGNETIC MAN. Berkley, 1968. THE AVENGERS
    #8. Based on television series.
THE MOON EXPRESS. Berkley, 1969. THE AVENGERS
    #9. Based on television series.
LAW OF THE LASH. Lancer, 1969.
THE KONO DIAMOND. Berkley, 1969.
STANTON BISHOP, M.D. Lancer, 1969.
MASTER OF WYNDWARD. Lancer 1969.
RAPE OF A TOWN. Pyramid, 1970.
JUBAL. Paperback Library, 1970.
THE PLUNDERERS. Ace, 1970.
THE SAVAGE HEART. Lancer 1970.
SLAVE REBELLION. Paperback Library, 1970.
ONE ANGRY MAN. Pyramid, 1971.
OPERATION S-L. Pyramid, 1971. THE MAN FROM
    A.P.E. series.
MEET THE SMITHS. Berkley, 1971. THE SMITH
    FAMILY #1. Based on television series.
LICENSE TO KILL. Pyramid, 1972.
BLACKWELL's GHOST. Lancer, 1972. As Angela
    Gray.
THE WARLOCK'S DAUGHTER. Lancer, 1972. As
    Angela Gray.
NIGHTMARE AT RIVERVIEW. Lancer 1973. As
    Angela Gray.
THE CHASE. Berkley, 1974. Based on television
    series.
WYNDWARD PASSION. Warner Books, 1978.
WYNDWARD FURY. Warner Books, 1979.
WYNDWARD PERIL. Warner Books, 1980.
WYNDWARD GLORY. To be published by Warner Books.

The following additional gothic novels appeared under female pseudonyms: Angela Gray, Helen Gray Weston, Cynthia Cavanaugh, Suzanne Somers, Daniella Dorsett, Helaine Ross, Geraldine Thayer. The books on the left, despite bylines, are all authored by Norman Daniels alone. The books on the right are collaborations with Dorothy Daniels.

CALDWELL SHADOW	AFFAIR IN HONG KONG
CHILD OF DARKNESS	BLUE DEVIL SUITE
CURSE OF MALLORY HALL	BRIDE OF LENORE
DANCE IN DARKNESS	THE DECEPTION
DUELING OAKS	HOUSE OF FALSE FACES
EXORCISM OF JENNY SLADE	ISLAND OF EVIL
THE DUNCAN DYNASTY	KNIGHT IN RED ARMOR
GHOST DANCERS	THE LANIER RIDDLE
GOLDEN PACKET	LAST OF THE MANSIONS
HOUSE OF BROKEN DOLLS	MISTS OF MOURNING
IMAGE OF A GHOST	MOSTLY BY MOONLIGHT
JADE GREEN	SCREEN TEST FOR LAUREL
MAYA TEMPLE	STRANGE PARADISE
POSSESSION OF TRACY CORBIN	SURVIVOR OF DARKNESS
PRISONER OF MALVILLE HALL	THIS ANCIENT EVIL
RAVENSWOOD HALL	TOWER ROOM
THE ROMANY CURSE	TRAITOR'S ROAD
TIDEMILL	THE UNGUARDED
TWO WORLDS OF PEGGY SCOTT	VOODOO PRIESTESS
THE UNEARTHLY	
UNTIL DEATH	
WATCHER IN THE DARK	

Dashiell Hammett in the Dell Mapbacks
by William Lyles

BLOOD MONEY. #53 A) U.S. Edition, ca. Sept. 1944: 170,000 copies; B) Canadian Edition, ca. Nov. 1945: 19,000 copies; C) U.S. Reissue, ca. July 1945: 75,000 copies. Front cover by Gerald Gregg; map by Ruth Belew.
#486:   March 1951: 200,000 copies (22,000 shipped to Canada). Fron cover by Robert Stanley; map probably by Ruth Belew. Original publication: as **$106,000 BLOOD MONEY** (Bestseller Mystery #B40, 1943).

A MAN CALLED SPADE and Other Stories [ed. Ellery Queen]. #90: A) U.S. Edition, ca. Nov. 1945: 202,000 copies; B) Canadian Edition, ca. May 1946: 24,749 copies. Front cover by Gerald Gregg or Otto Storch; map by Ruth Belew.
#411:   July 1950: 201,500 copies (20,000 shipped to Canada). Front cover by Robert Stanley; same map as on #90.
#452: November 1950: 201,000 copies (22,000 shipped to Canada). Same cover and map as on #411.
Original publication: as **THE ADVENTURES OF SAM SPADE AND OTHER STORIES** (Bestseller Myster #B50, 1944), later as **THEY CAN ONLY HANG YOU ONCE.**

THE CONTINENTAL OP [ed. Ellery Queen].   #129: A) U.S. Edition, ca. Oct. 1946: 251,000 copies; B) Canadian Edition, ca. April 1947: 19,860 copies. Front cover by Gregg; map by Belew. Original publication: Bestseller Mystery #B62, 1945.

THE RETURN OF THE CONTINENTAL OP [ed. Ellery Queen]. #154:   A) U.S. Edition, ca. March 1947: 200,000 copies; B) Canadian Edition, ca. February 1948: 20,845 copies. Front cover by Gregg; map by Belew.
Original publication: Bestseller Mystery #B81, 1946.

HAMMETT HOMICIDES, ed. Ellery Queen. #223: A) U.S. Edition, ca. May 1948: 201,000 copies; B) Canadian Edition, ca. November 1948: 19,745 copies. Front cover by Gregg; map by Belew.
Original publication: Bestseller Mystery #B81, 1946.

DEAD YELLOW WOMEN. #308: ca. Sept. 1949: 150,000 copies. Front cover by Gregg; map probably by Belew.
#421: A) ca. May 1950: 14,637 copies; B) reissue, ca. July 1950: 62,500 copies. Same cover & map as on #308.
Original publication: Jonathan Press Mystery #J29, 1947.

NIGHTMARE TOWN, ed. Ellery Queen [illus. by Lester Elliot]. #379: ca. February 1950: 277,000 copies. Front cover by Robert Stanley; map probably by Belew.
Original publication: Mercury Mystery #120, 1948.

THE CREEPING SIAMESE, ed. Ellery Queen. #538: Sept. 1951: 305,000 copies (21,800 shipped to Canada). Front cover by Robert Stanley; map probably by Belew.
Original publication: Jonathan Press Mystery #J48, 1950.

Front & Back Covers of *Blood Money*, Dell #53

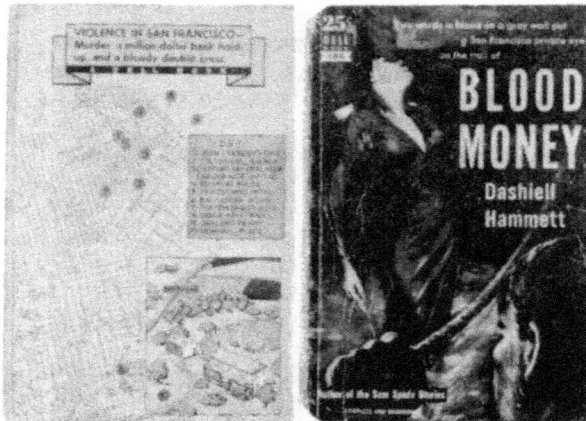

Front & Back Covers of *Blood Money*, Dell #486

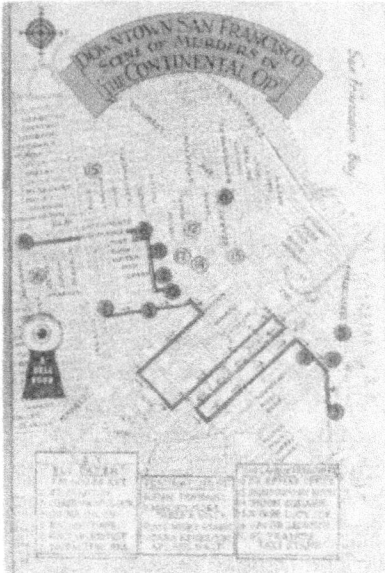

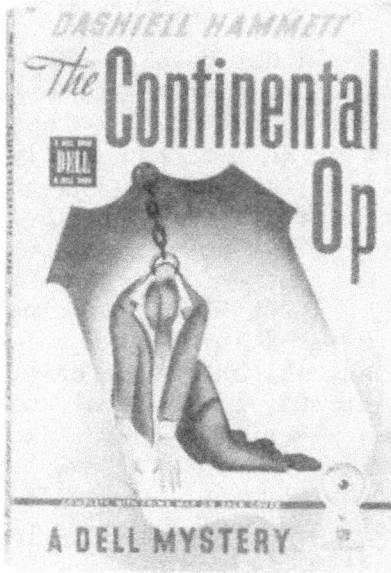

Front & Back Covers of *The Continental Op*, Dell #129

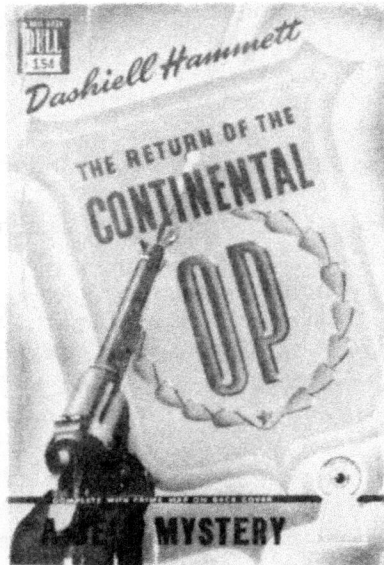

Front & Back Covers of *The Return of the Continental Op*, Dell #154

17

Samuel Dashiel Hammett (1894-1961), the most famous writer of hard-boiled mysteries, needs no introduction here. But although readers of Hammett can easily find his works in print, they may be unaware of a very attractive, collectible series of Dell "mapback" editions of one of his novels and seven collections of his stories.

BLOOD MONEY, originally published as two stories ("The Big Knockover" and "$106,000 Blood Money"), may not be Hammett's best novel, but it certainly towers over most of the thrillers written since the 1930s. It is a good introduction to The Continental Op, Hammett's nameless, lumpy private detective (called "Percy Maguire," a sort of adopted nom de guerre, in the character list of #53). The front cover of #53, a slick Gerald Gregg airbrushed arrangement of primary colors, reflects the tight, precise prose of Hammett and suggests the unpretentious violence of the book. (A comparatively limp variation of this cover adorns the contemporary Vintage paperback edition.) Robert Stanley's cover for #486, on the other hand, suggests a rather romantic novel; interested readers will find the incident depicted on page 141 of the latter edition. The map of #53, devoted entirely to Ann Newhall's country residence south of San Francisco, depicts a locale which figures only late in the book; #453 intelligently places the Newhall residence as an inset in a larger map of San Francisco, a map helpful for those who believe New York (or worse, Los Angeles) is the center of the known civilized world.

A MAN CALLED SPADE collects a fine group of stories, none of which, unfortunately, really demand a map. The map on all the Dell editions derives from the title story: it depicts Apt. #10K (of Max Bliss) on Nob Hill, in San Francisco. Unfortunately, the staff who colored the map did not pay attention to precise colors, since the secrétaire is not green,

18

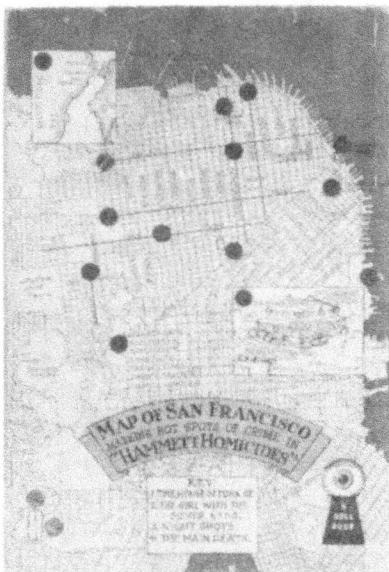

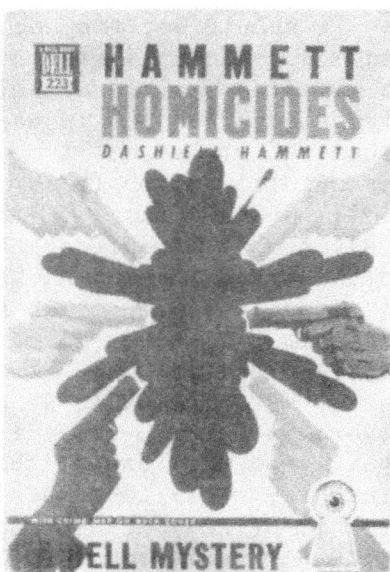

Front & Back Covers of *Hammett Homicides*, Dell #223

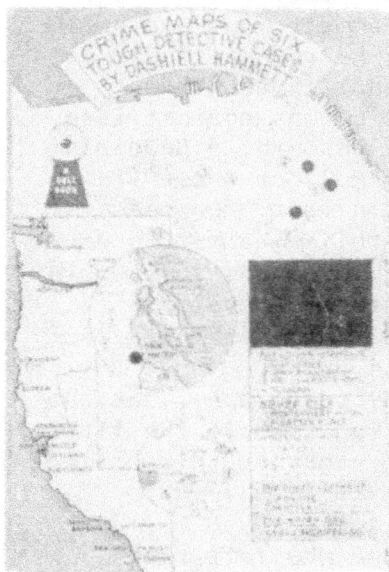

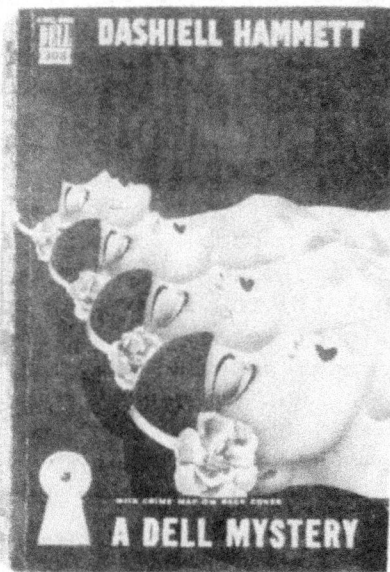

Front & Back Covers of *Dead Yellow Women*, Dell #308

as it should be, the necktie not blue, and so on. Such details assume greater importance on a map of a small area such as this one. The front cover of #90 is an interesting twisting scene of violence; it may be the only Dell cover by Otto Storch (a former art director for Dell in New York). The identical covers on #411 and #452 represent Robert Stanley's version of Sam Spade: no "blond Satan," perhaps, (see page 41), but then neither was Humphrey Bogart. The cover illustrates page 72 of the story "They Can Only Hang You Once."

THE CONTINENTAL OP cover is a brilliant exercise in color, but I have no idea what it has to do with any of the stories. A person recently wrote to me asking me to list and quote to him prices for all paperback covers dealing with strangulation. This must be what he had in mind. (For reasons I hope are obvious, I never replied.) The map is much better: excellent and helpful, fun to use. Jim Hawkins, a former employee of Western Printing & Lithographing, used to check the Hammett maps against the author's descriptions; he remembers Hammet's San Francisco as extraordinarily accurate. (Hawkins checked the descriptions against Esso maps, also printed then by Western.) Readers might find interesting the McCloor chase (in orange) from "Fly Paper"; in fact, few readers would probably be able to follow Hammett's descriptions without the map. Perhaps some would not try to, preferring character development alone, yet they might lose the excitement topography assumes in Hammett's prose.

For those left cold by topography, but who still appreciate fine writing, sample the first two paragraphs of the last story in this collection, "The Farewell Murder":

I was the only one who left the train at Farewell.
A man came through the rain from

20

> the passenger shed. He was a small
> man. His face was dark and flat. He
> wore a gray waterproof cap and a gray
> coat in military fashion.

Could any mystery reader not follow up those
leads?

THE RETURN OF THE CONTINENTAL OP, another
superb collection, has an ordinary, disappointing cover; but an extremely helpful map. Unfortunately, the color-coded banners intrude rather
than aid in some cases, especially since the
distinction between the light purple (for "One
Hour") and orange (for "The Tenth Clue") is
slight.

The explicit cover of HAMMETT HOMICIDES
features a characteristic riot of Gregg's air-
brush variety. But while the map is useful
here, the arrangement is confusing: I have no
idea what the many "4's" on the map correspond
to in "The Main Death." And while the characters listed on the first page are in the order
in which they appear in the stories (as are the
characters in the lists of the other Dell editions), the order of "Things..." and the teasers
in "Wouldn't You Like to Know" are jumbled up--
a challenge, perhaps, to the detective-reader.

DEAD YELLOW WOMEN is a stunning Gregg cover; the original, which I saw in the artist's
home, is even more vibrant and vivid than the
reproduction. The map appears elaborate and
complex; actually, it is disappointing in its
omissions and errors. For example, the purple
#2 (Pigatti's Place) refers to two stories, yet
the color codes it to only one; and in the
fourth story, Ogburn's apartment should not be
located in San Francisco (perhaps the artist
meant Police Headquarters--Sacramento--as #4
but mislabelled it). Hammett readers should
approach this edition with caution.

They can approach NIGHTMARE TOWN with
wonder--that is, to wonder why the back cover

21

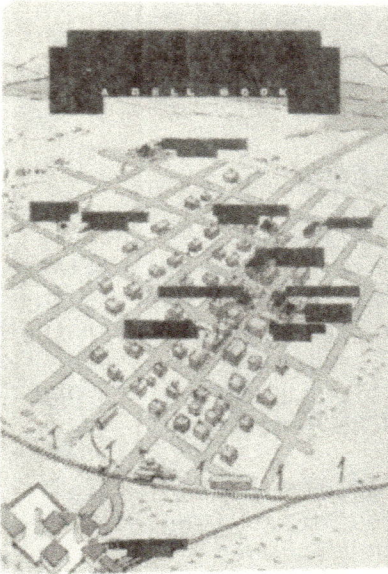

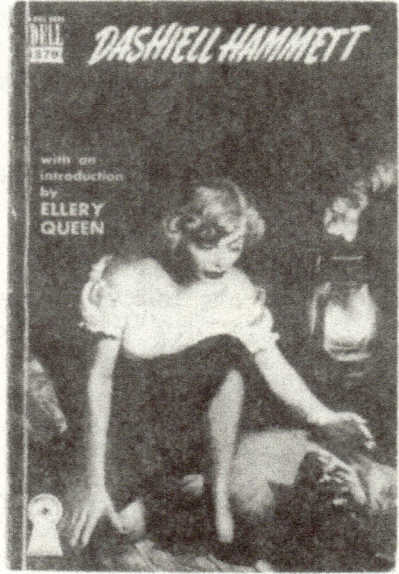

Front & Back Covers of *Nightmare Town*, Dell #379

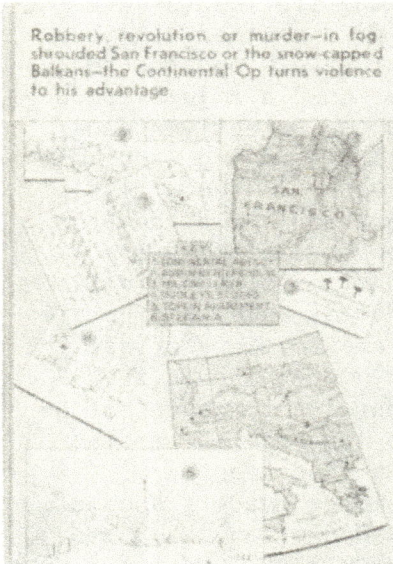

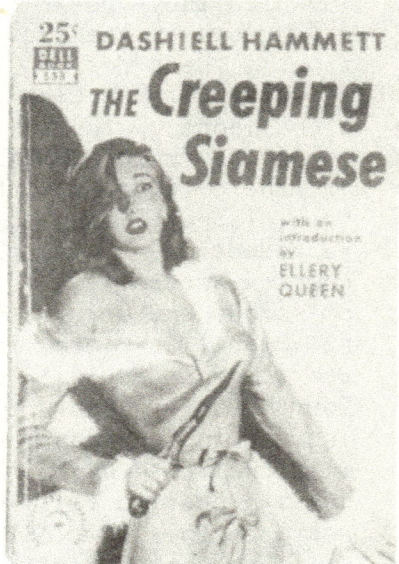

Front & Back Covers of *The Creeping Siamese*, Dell #538

is graced by a map of "Izzard in the Desert,"
which refers only to the title story, and not
a map of San Francisco, which would be partic-
ularly useful here, especially in connection
with "The Scorched Place." Yet those who find
the map too unrealistic a depiction of a town
(even a desert town) should reserve judgment
until reaching pages 53-56 of the title story.
I am not precisely sure what Stanley's cover
illustrates; can anyone enlighten me?

THE CREEPING SIAMESE, the last Dell collection of Hammett stories features another Stanley cover. Anyone who finds Stanley's work
rather familiar after this time probably does
so because of the recurring figures: he used
two models most of the time--himself (Sam Spade,
for example), and his wife, Rhoda (here holding
the dagger--see page 24). The map provides an
attractive but useless montage of places, the
last (#6) illustrating the Op's most unusual
locale, the fictitious Balkan country, Stefania.
Readers who think they "know" Hammett may find
interesting a reading of "The Nails in Mr.
Cayterer," which features a competent but de-
cidedly effeminate detective--quite different
from the Op.

Two other collections of Hammett stories
were published: WOMAN IN THE DARK and A MAN
CALLED THIN. Dell had an option on the first.
Dell also planned a 10¢ edition of the story,
"The Girl with Silver Eyes" (from HAMMETT HOMI-
CIDES); artist Victor Kalin remembers completing
a painting for the cover. But the 10¢ series
was disbanded after less than a year.

References:

Layman, Richard. DASHIELL HAMMETT: A DE-
SCRIPTIVE BIBLIOGRAPHY ([Pittsburgh]: Universi-
ty of Pittsburgh Press, 1979).
Nolan, William F. DASHIELL HAMMETT: A
CASEBOOK (Santa Barbara: McNally & Loftin, 1969).

SF Writers in Other Fields
by Bill Crider

What makes a paperback book collectible? Lots of things, obviously, but one thing that determines value in many cases is the author of the book. It's always fun to run across an offbeat book by a particular writer, one who's being collected because he specialized in books of a type different from the one you've found.

A good example of what I'm talking about are non-sf books by writers generally known for their science fiction work. Probably the most collectible of these writers is Harlan Ellison, who once wrote a pretty good book about a rock star--"Stag Preston, idol of millions"--which he called SPIDER KISS and which Gold Medal published as ROCKABILLY in 1961. The Hooks cover for the GM edition isn't bad, but the back cover photo of Ellison is even better. I didn't know that he smoked (and I guess he doesn't, now). Ellison also did some work in the juvenile delinquent field, with THE JUVIES (Ace, 1961) and RUMBLE (Pyramid, 1958, 1963)-- "Harlan Ellison joined one of the toughest gangs in New York to find out what their life was really like. The result is RUMBLE."

For some reason, people tend to think of Harlan Ellison and Isaac Asimov together. Asimov also did a few non-sf paperbacks, not counting non-fiction and such things as THE SENSUOUS DIRTY OLD MAN by "Dr. A." What I'm thinking of are his mysteries, like THE DEATH DEALERS (Avon, 1958), billed by the publishers as Asimov's "mystery-writing debut." I suppose THE CAVES OF STEEL and THE NAKED SUN don't count. THE DEATH DEALERS was later reprinted by Lancer as A WHIFF OF DEATH in an undated 95¢ edition, with (as far as I can tell) no acknowledgement whatever on the cover or the copyright page that it was ever printed under another title.

One of the more interesting works of the sort

by Harlan Ellison

by Robert Graham

by Fritz Leiber

by Isaac Asimov

I'm discussing, and one of the more difficult to
find, is Fritz Leiber's THE SINFUL ONES; at least
it's hard to find in its original edition, being
one half of Uni Giant #5 (the other half being
BULLS, BLOOD AND PASSION). In fact, THE SINFUL
ONES has only recently been reprinted in paperback
and for years the Uni edition was the only one
available.

Another collectible author is Jack Vance.
Not counting his Ellery Queen mysteries (and there
are lots of Ellery Queen fans who are glad not to
count them), he's done at least one paperback
original mystery under his full name of John
Holbrook Vance. As BAD RONALD was published by
Ballantine in 1973, it shouldn't be too hard to
find, but some collectors seem to put a pretty
high value on it.

Monarch Books, according to Bill Pronzini,
published sf by virtually unknown writers while
issuing non-sf books by men well known for their
sf books. Examples include Mack Reynolds' suspense novel, EPISODE ON THE RIVIERA (1969) and
Poul Anderson's nonfiction THERMONUCLEAR WARFARE
(1963).

You can also find sf writers hiding behind
pseudonyms, or behind their real names. Will F.
Jenkins, better known to sf readers as Murray
Leinster, did several westerns as Jenkins, including Gold Medal's movie tie-in DALLAS (1950).
Robert Vardeman, probably best-known for his col-
laborative effort, the "War of the Powers" series,
or for his recent Star Trek novel, is the Nick
Carter of Charter's EIGHTH CARD STUD (1980). And
Joe Haldeman said at one sf convention in 1981
that the book he most enjoyed writing was WAR OF
NERVES (Pocket, 1975), which was the second book
in the "Attar the Merman" series produced by the
ubiquitous Lyle Kenyon Engle. Haldeman did both
books in the series, which ended with the second,
under the name of Robert Graham.

All these books are fun to own. Most of them
are fun to read.

by Poul Anderson

by Mack Reynolds

by Will F. Jenkins

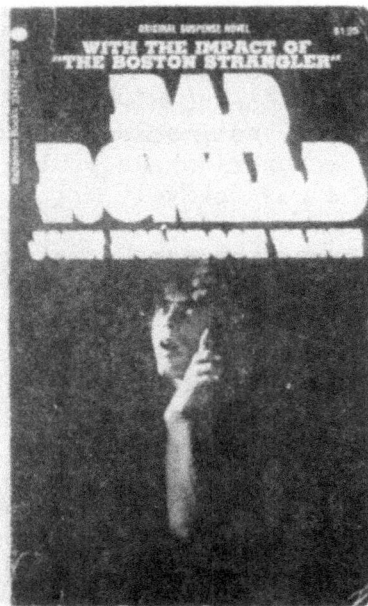

by John Holbrook Vance

Eugene Manlove Rhodes
by M.C. Hill

It's a sad commentary on our times, but
nevertheless the truth, that the output of some
of our greatest writers of the past have been
relegated to the archives of some of our largest
libraries, museums, and publishers' record
vaults.

With new writers appearing on the scene
daily, having their books publicized by news-
papers, television specials, author signing and
promotion parties, etc., no wonder the past is
buried under tons of new material, which in
many cases is far inferior to that which has
already met with proven success.

It is true that great writers of the past
such as Zane Grey, Luke Short, Max Brand, J.
Frank Dobie, Jack London, Stanley Vestal, and
Eugene Cunningham are kept in print because of
name-recognition and demand. But many other
fine writers are only available in the paperbacks of the 1940s and 1950s.

One such writer is Eugene Manlove Rhodes.
In my estimation, his books never received the
recognition and publicity they deserved. When
he was actively writing (1900-1920), writers'
agents or representatives had not yet become
a part of the normal writer/publisher relation-
ship. Each writer had to uncover and promote
himself within his own market, and Rhodes was
a victim of his own inadequacies in pushing
himself into the right markets. Having become
associated with small, unknown publishing
houses such as Fly, his works did not at first
reach large audiences.

Henry Holt, Grossett and Dunlap, and
Houghton Mifflin did publish some of his writings, but always in limited numbers of from
3,000 to 23,000, with the average running from

4,000 to 6,000 copies. Consequently, these books are very difficult to locate today.

Another factor in Rhodes' lack of popular success is that he did not write the usual shoot-em-up action story but western historical fiction that concentrated on the lives of his characters. He used many of his close associates in many of his stories and set his stories in actual locations. In all respects, his stories have the ring of authenticity.

Rhodes was born in Tecumseh, Nebraska in 1869. When he was twelve, his parents moved to New Mexico, seeking a better life. He attended school in New Mexico and worked as a cowboy and rancher. Eventually he went to college in California and later became a teacher. He fled New Mexico because of an incident in which some cattle belonging to his neighbor were killed. He claimed it was a mistake, but he was blamed. For the next twenty years, he lived in the East, not returning to New Mexico until the statute of limitations ran out.

When he finally returned, he had become an established writer in a dozen prominent magazines, including THE SATURDAY EVENING POST. He wrote about what he knew with vigor, wit and humor. During his 38 years as a writer he produced over 130 stories and novelettes, as well as articles, essays, poems, books and serials. Many were written while staring at the proverbial wolf at the door, or while Rhodes was so ill he could hardly sit up. Suffering many hardships himself, he used his writings to champion the forgotten, down-trodden, and underdogs who fought against the odds to satisfy the desire for equality and justice.

As a writer, he was known and respected by such men as J. Frank Dobie, Charles Russell, Ross Santee, and Will James.

His readers are deeply indebted to W. H. Hutchinson, who spent many years gathering his letters, books, magazines, articles and poems

by Eugene Manlove Rhodes

Eugene Manlove Rhodes

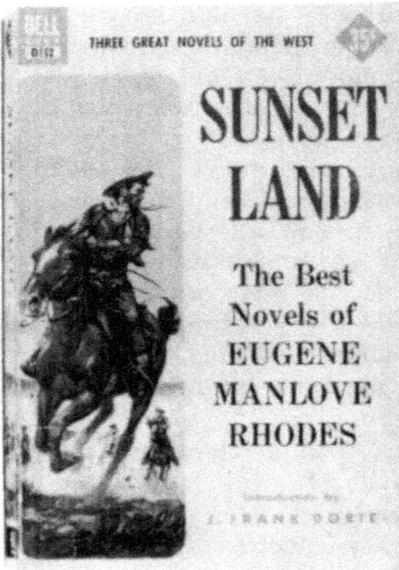

by Eugene Manlove Rhodes

and contacting Rhodes' family, friends and associates. Hutchinson's research culminated in the
publication of THE LIFE AND PERSONAL WRITINGS OF
EUGENE MANLOVE RHODES: A BAR CROSS MAN by
University of Oklahoma Press.

I hope that a paperback publisher will
reissue Rhodes' writings for a world that needs
the strength, stability, integrity and fearless-
ness that they depict so convincingly. Until
that happens, readers, as well as collectors,
will have to search out his paperback publications of the 1940s and 1950s because his early
hardback books are nearly impossible to find.
Five of his stories were reprinted in the famous
Armed Services Editions, and two were issued by
Dell. His story, "The Fool's Heart" appeared in
three anthologies. It is disappointing that
editors kept presenting the same story when they
could have used any number of equally good
Rhodes stories.

Following is as complete a list of Rhodes'
paperback appearances as I can compile. If
anyone knows of any others, I would appreciate
the information.

Pocket Book #117 POCKET BOOK OF MYSTERY STORIES
    (contains "The Fool's Heart") August 1941.
Hillman #44 THE TRUSTY KNAVES
Hillman #46 COPPER STREAK TRAIL
Armed Services Editions:
    G-190 THE TRUSTY KNAVES (50,000 copies)
           May 1944
    H-212 BEYOND THE DESERT (68,000 copies)
           June 1944
    J-271 THE PROUD SHERIFF (68,000 copies)
           August 1944
    K-8   STEPSONS OF LIGHT (68,000 copies)
           September 1944
    M-6   COPPER STREAK TRAIL (68,000 copies)
           November 1944
Pocket Book #293 POCKET BOOK OF WESTERN STORIES
    (contains "Beyond the Desert") March 1945

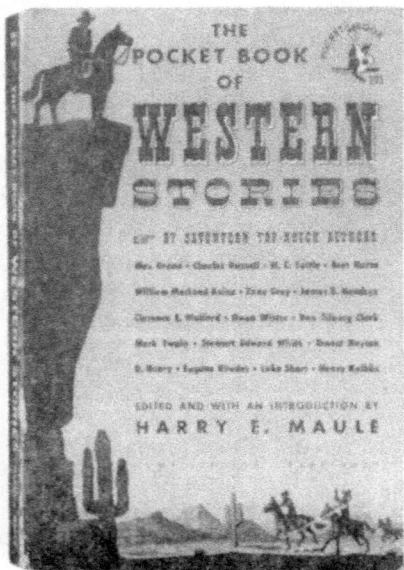

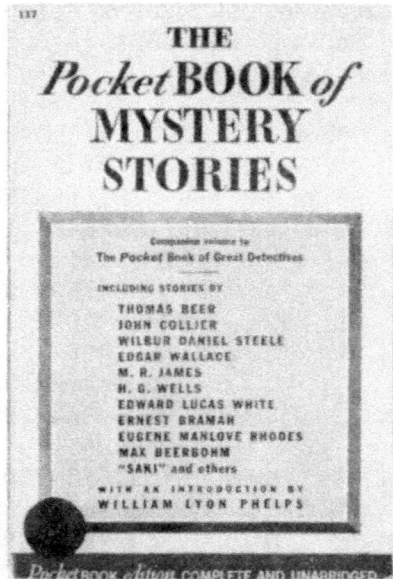

Paperback Anthologies with Stories by Eugene Manlove Rhodes

Bantam #256 WESTERN ROUNDUP (contains "The
    Long Shift") September 1948
Dell #367 SUSPENSE STORIES (contains "The
    Fool's Heart") 1950; reissued as Dell
    #1367
Dell #688 THE PROUD SHERIFF, with a 38-page
    introduction by H. H. Knibbs, 1953
Dell #D152 SUNSET LAND (collection of three
    stories: "Good Men and True," "Bransford
    of Rainbow Range" (formerly titled "Little
    Eohippus"), and "The Trusty Knaves") with
    a 22-page introduction by J. Frank Dobie,
    August 1955
Popular Library #M2086 POST READER OF WESTERN
    STORIES (contains "The Fool's Heart"),
    1960
Dell #3626 ALFRED HITCHCOCK'S A BAKER'S DOZEN
    OF SUSPENCE STORIES (contains "The Fool's
    Heart"), December 1963

Two other Rhodes' stories appeared in digest-
form. The first was brought to my attention by
David Bates, who is doing a book on the Dell
digest-size western magazine.

ZANE GREY'S WESTERN MAGAZINE, December 1947
    (contains "Bell the Cat")
ZANE GREY'S WESTERN MAGAZINE, March 1947
    (contains "Wizard of Finance")

Following is a list of books about Eugene
Manlove Rhodes.

THE HIRED MAN ON HORSEBACK (Boston: Houghton,
    Mifflin Co., 11 September 1938) by May D.
    Rhodes. (two printings; 3,000 copies sold)
THE BEST NOVELS AND STORIES OF EUGENE MANLOVE
    RHODES (Boston: Houghton, Mifflin Co.,
    1949) edited by F. V. Dearing. (6,000
    copies)
THE LIFE AND PERSONAL WRITINGS OF EUGENE

MANLOVE RHODES: A BAR CROSS MAN (Norman,
Oklahoma: University of Oklahoma Press,
1956) by W. H. Hutchinson
GENE RHODES, COWBOY (New York: Julian Messner,
September 1954) by Beth F. Day

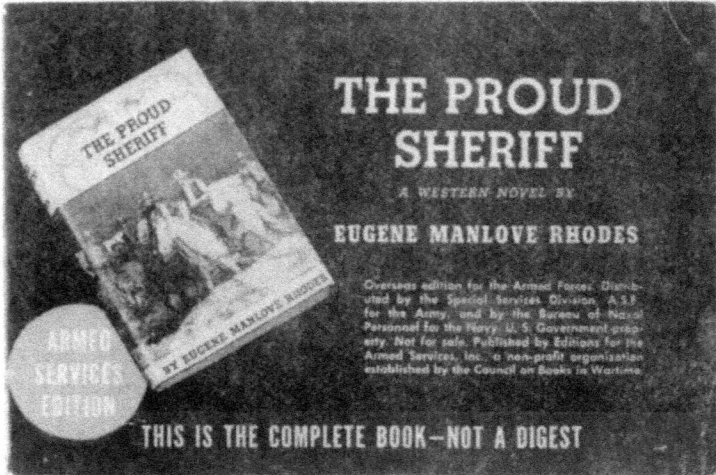

THE PROUD SHERIFF
A WESTERN NOVEL BY
EUGENE MANLOVE RHODES

Overseas edition for the Armed Forces. Distributed by the Special Services Division, A.S.F. for the Army, and by the Bureau of Naval Personnel for the Navy. U. S. Government property. Not for sale. Published by Editions for the Armed Services, Inc., a non-profit organization established by the Council on Books in Wartime.

THIS IS THE COMPLETE BOOK—NOT A DIGEST

Covers That Never Were

The following are two covers by Robert
Jonas, for Penguin 627: LIGHTHOUSE by Archie
Binns, and Bantam 35: A FAREWELL TO ARMS by
Ernest Hemingway. Before you run to your
bookshelves to check the numbers on these two
extremely rare paperbacks, you might as well
know the truth: the books do not exist. These
reproductions were made from press-proofs that
are in Robert Jonas' possession. They are
finished covers, but the books themselves never
appeared in this form. Penguin 627 was TOBACCO
ROAD (also, incidentally, with a Jonas cover);
Bantam 35 was MY DEAR BELLA by Arthur Kober
(with a cover by Thomas Ruzicka and Sydney Hoff).
A color reproduction of the A FAREWELL TO
ARMS cover may be seen on page 71 of Piet
Schreuders' PAPERBACKS, U.S.A.

The Pocket Books/De Graff Formula
by Charley Culpepper

In an advertisement in the October 31, 1980 PUBLISHERS WEEKLY, Pocket Books claimed to have invented the paperback book in 1939. In his book on the history of paperback books Frank Schick wrote that the publication of Pocket Books in 1939 marked the beginning of the paperback revolution and that it was their approach to distribution rather than the publication of inexpensive paperbound books which has to be considered the radical departure from past practices by Pocket Books.[1]

These comments by Dr. Schick are typical of what has been said about the achievement of Pocket Books. A "paperback revolution" is not a tangible or a specific description. What specifically did Pocket Books do in 1939 that Penguin hadn't done in 1935 or Modern Age, American Mercury Books or Mystery Novel of the Month in 1937 or 1938? Did Pocket Books do less than it is usually credited with? Did they do more? Did they really invent the paperback?

To clarify the achievement of Pocket Books it is necessary to put it in the context of book publishing in the 1920s and 1930s.[2]

These were times in book publishing which saw continuous experimentation in pricing and merchandising in an attempt to reach a wider market of buyers by reducing prices. A true mass market for books was developing in the U. S. with the rapid increase in population, the shift from a rural to an urban population, and a decline in the rate of illiteracy.[3]

Some of the means publishers were using to try to reach this developing mass market were book clubs, subscription sales, hardcover reprints, remainders, rental libraries, and paperback experiments. Reprint book publishers were trying to woo magazine readers with reduced prices and reach them through the magazine distribution system with its 80,000 sales outlets in the mid-1930s (up from 50,000 in 1915)[4] compared to less than 3,000 trade book outlets. After all, the SATURDAY EVENING POST sold more copies a year than the entire book industry.

One publisher who realized that the possibilities of book distribution had barely been scratched was Frank N. Doubleday, founder of the firm FORTUNE called the "selling machine" in a February 1936 article. In the 1920s Frank Doubleday constantly explored new means of gaining mass readership. His son Nelson succeeded him and did the same thing in the 1930s. Nelson Doubleday's intention was to sell books to people who had never before bought books, something he felt could be done more easily with reprints or established books at a lower price than with new books at regular prices.[5]

Robert Fair de Graff, cousin of Nelson Doubleday (Nelson's mother's maiden name was de Graff), had gone to work for Doubleday in 1922 as a salesman. By 1925 he was vice president and director of Garden City Publishing Company, a Doubleday subsidiary and a leader in the reprint field, where he originated and marketed 15 million Star Dollar Books. Resigning in 1936, he became president of another reprint leader, Blue Ribbon Books, where he developed Triangle Books, a new series of fiction reprints that sold for 39¢ each.[6]

According to John Tebbel, an authority on book publishing history, de Graff was perhaps the most experienced man in the reprint field when he resigned from Blue Ribbon Books in 1938 to start Pocket Books.[7]

In May 1939, after supplementing his experience and knowledge of book publishing with further study and market research, de Graff implemented what proved to be a very successful formula: editorial selection, 25¢ price, pocket size, attractive multi-color covers, low-cost printing using high-speed rotary presses (magazine printing), and distribution through news-stands and other

37

outlets used by magazines.

By the end of 1939 Pocket Books had published
34 titles which had sold over 1½ million copies.
In 1940 they published 53 titles which sold 4½
million copies.[8] In 1944 Pocket Books sold 35
million copies; and the company, which had been
started five years before on an investment of
$60,000, was sold to Marshall Field for $3 million,
with de Graff remaining on as head.[9] After 10
years in business Pocket Books had issued 600
titles which had sold 260 million copies; 56 titles
had sold in excess of one million copies each.
Pocket Books claimed 260 million copies was more
than the combined total of all best sellers published since 1880, including all major book club
selections and all reprints other than Pocket
Books.[10]

What were the specific achievements of
Pocket Books and Robert de Graff?

(1.) Pocket Books introduced a formula that
was largely followed by other successful mass-
distribution paperback publishers such as Avon,
Dell, Popular Library, and Bantam.

The establishment of a mass-distribution
system is usually emphasized at the expense of the
other elements in the formula. But the parts of
de Graff's letter to Frank Schick that are quoted
in the latter's book indicate that de Graff himself
considered the other elements vital.

For example, de Graff says that the Boni
paperback books were definitely a quality product
physically "but did not have the editorial selection adequate to insure its success."[11]

In another example he tells of his experience
as manager of Star Dollar Books (these were the
first successful non-fiction hardback reprints,
incidentally). De Graff says the books didn't sell
because the original jackets were of "semi-uniform
design and not attractive enough." But when he had
the books rejacketed with appealing pictorial
covers, 15 million books were sold.[12]

A final example concerns reprint paperback

books that Garden City Publishing Company, the Doubleday subsidiary, had created, without success, to compete with Street & Smith in the 1920s. De Graff wrote that the books retailed for 25¢ but were "duodecimo in size and bulky"[13] and did not compare in value with clothbound remainder books of the same price.

One way to assess the value of the elements of the formula is to compare the successful Pocket Books/de Graff formula with the efforts of Penguin, American Mercury Books, Mystery Novel of the Month, Modern Age and Red Arrow, all of whom were publishing paperbacks in 1939.

In 1937 and 1938, in an attempt to obtain mass distribution American Mercury Books, Mystery Novel of the Month and Modern Age all started with magazine distribution, as Pocket Books did in 1939. But the former two were much more limited in categories of subjects and they published only one title a month or every other month. American Mercury Books originally published one title bi-monthly with a limited range of categories and later switched to one title a month and to mysteries exclusively. Mystery Novel of the Month published one title a month, all mysteries.

Modern Age published multi-titles monthly, over 90 in less than three years, and published as wide a variety of categories as Pocket Books did. But the Modern Age titles were less saleable and over 30 of the first 52 were originals instead of reprints. Several commentators have said that Modern Age's titles were too highbrow for mass distribution outlets. After less than a year, Modern Age switched from mass to trade distribution; and by the end of 1939, they were out of the paperback business.[14] Like American Mercury Books and Mystery Novel of the Month, Modern Age was digest in size, approximately 5 5/8 by 7 5/8. Digest-sized books were often stacked up in newsstands one on top of the other rather than being displayed in wire racks as "pocket-size" paperbacks were.

Penguin published its first 10 titles in
1935 and after four successful years it opened
up an American branch two months after Pocket
Books had distributed its first 10 titles.
Penguin began its U. S. Operations with trade
distribution only and with bright and colorful
but non-pictorial covers.[15] However, Ian Ballantine, observing the success of Pocket Books,
later changed to mass distribution and to pictorial covers.

Red Arrow published 12 titles in the fall of
1939 using some of the de Graff formula (magazine
printing and distribution, 25¢ price, a mixture
of mystery, general fiction and adventure subjects) but they lacked several ingredients. The
books were unattractive in appearance, with dull
colors, and most covers had a blurb but no picture.
Even their Penquin-size did not look good. Having more pages and being thicker, they did not
have the thin sleekness of Penguin but looked
bulky and clumsy instead. They apparently realized part of their mistake and rejacketed several titles in brightly colored pictorial covers.
After publication of their first 12 titles, Red
Arrow published no more paperback books.

(2.) Pocket Books initiated the gradual
takeover of the hardback reprint business by
the paperback, a reversal of what Grossett and
Dunlap had done at the turn of the century.[16]

Ultimately, this led to the virtual takeover of the book business by the paperback. A
survey published by PUBLISHERS WEEKLY in January
1981 revealed that nearly 70% of unit book sales
in 1980 were paperbacks, 41% mass distribution
and 28% trade. Gradually in the 1940s the
established hardback reprint leaders lost out to
Pocket Books and the other paperback companies.
Grossett and Dunlap, the reprint leader during
most of the first four decades of this century,
had lost most of its reprint business by the

mid-1940s.[17] Doubleday's Triangle Books, another
reprint leader, which de Graff himself had
started when president of Blue Ribbon Books, was
out of business by the late 1940s.[18] Even such
a well-established series as Modern Library, one
of the most successful ventures in publishing
history, was hurt and eventually faded away.

(3.) Pocket Books didn't merely expand
paperback books to a mass distribution system,
they expanded the reprint book market to a mass
distribution basis, bringing in millions of new
people as book buyers for the first time. They
reached that wider audience the book industry
had sought continuously throughout the first four
decades of the century through reprints and other
means.

When Pocket Books began in 1939, de Graff
used the American News Company for distribution,
a firm which had been the major distributor of
magazines for about 90 years. Dissatisfied with
A. N. C., de Graf began setting up a distribution
system through Independent Distributors (IDs) and
had 600 by 1941.[19] It was at this point that it
is generally accepted that the first true mass
distribution system was in operation.

It is interesting to note that three of
Pocket Books' major competitors--Dell, Avon and
Popular Library--used A. N. C. for their distribution throughout the 1940s.[20] And they did pretty
well.

Also, Freeman Lewis, an executive with de
Graff at Blue Ribbon Books who later joined him
at Pocket Books, said in 1952 that 80% of all
sales came through 30,000 of the 110,000 sales
outlets Pocket Books and its competitors were
using in the early 1950s.[21]

Comments about the achievement of Pocket Books
are too often limited to the context of paperback
books (e.g., the paperback revolution, the mass-
distribution paperback) whereas the true impact
has been on the entire book industry, not just on

41

paperbacks. A study I made of three major sources of publishing history (Cited in the footnotes to this article) convinced me that no other change in 20th century publishing had a greater impact on the industry or the reading public than the changes brought about by what Robert de Graff and Pocket Books started in 1939. Perhaps nothing could say it better than what Pocket Books went on to say in the same ad when it said that in 1939 Pocket Books "reinvented" the book.

FOOTNOTES

[1]Frank L. Schick, THE PAPERBOUND BOOK IN AMERICA (New York: R. R. Bowker Company, 1958).

[2]Three excellent sources for information on 1920s and 1930s book publishing are John Tebbel's A HISTORY OF BOOK PUBLISHING IN THE UNITED STATES, Vol. III (New York: R. R. Bowker Company, 1978; Charles Madison's BOOK PUBLISHING IN AMERICA (New York: McGraw-Hill Book Company, 1966); Hellmut Lehmann-Haupt's THE BOOK IN AMERICA: A HISTORY OF THE MAKING AND SELLING OF BOOKS IN THE UNITED STATES, 2nd edition (New York: R. R. Bowker Company, 1951).

[3]Tebbel, p. 3.

[4]Tebbel, p. 103.

[5]Madison, p. 288.

[6]Tebbel, p. 508.

[7]Tebbel, p. 508.

[8]Freeman Lewis, "Paper-bound Books in America" BOWKER LECTURES ON BOOK PUBLISHING (New York: R. R. Bowker Company, 1957), p. 311.

[9]Tebbel, p. 510.

[10]Lehmann-Haupt, p. 351.

[11]Schick, p. 125.

[12]Schick, p. 127.

[13]Schick, p. 126.

[14]Tebbel, p. 506.

[15]Schick, p. 138.

[16]Full Circle: In 1898 while on a sales trip to New England an idea occurred to the co-partner

of a fledgling publishing company that was to
start this firm off on the road to becoming the
first hardback reprint company and the leading
reprint book company for the next 40 years.
George T. Dunlap, of the then Dunlap and Grossett
(the name was changed to Grossett and Dunlap when
the firm was re-formed and incorporated in 1900),
was waiting to see the buyer at the Shepard Company in Providence when his attention was drawn
to a stack of about 200 paperback copies of Hall
Craine's THE CHRISTIAN, a popular fiction novel.
The idea occurred to Dunlap that if he could re-
bind this paperback book that was selling for 39¢
in cloth covers and offer it for 50¢ that it would
sell a lot more copies than it would in paperback.
And he was right, for that idea was the start of
a change in book reprints from paperback to hardback.

About forty years later another man decided
that if he published reprints in paperback for
25¢ that more copies could be sold than of 39¢
hardback reprints. And he was right, for Robert
de Graff's idea converted the reprint book business
from almost entirely hardback to almost entirely
paperback, just as Dunlap's idea 40 years earlier
led to the conversion of the reprint business from
paperback to hard back. And it had come full circle.

[17] AT RANDOM: THE REMINISCENCES OF BENNETT
CERF (New York: Random Hsuse, 1977), p. 195.
     [18] Schick, p. 180.
    [19] Schick, pp. 104 & 129.
    [20] Lewis, p. 313.
    [21] Lewis, p. 313.

Paperback Postcards

by Thomas Bonn

Postcards featuring paperback cover art now join original art, posters, and calendars as spinoffs of paperback book collecting. Galas' Exotic Novel Cards issues a series of eight "Color Bookcover Cards," each displaying a cover from a pulp digest of the late forties/ early fifties era. Three of the illustrations in this series can be attributed to well-known paperback cover artists, Robert Schultz (SLUM DOCTOR), George Gross (BOY MADNESS), and Rodewald (VERNA IS A TRAMP).

Shot from a personal collection, the photographs vary in the quality of the reproduction as well as in the condition of the cover photographed. Curious triangles cover the imprint logo of six of the eight. Before being photographed, covers on which removed sticker prices exposed the white undercover were given color touch-ups. Uneven trimming cut a couple of cards at crooked angles.

Yet for all these defects the cards somehow have a charm and seem appropriate reminders of the original digests. Although not something to send on Mother's Day, these cards would be welcomed by fellow collectors with whom you correspond.

A set of 12 "Color Bookcover Cards" sells for $6.00. Dealers' rates are available, and dealers are expected to place a minimum order for $35.00. Inquiries should be addressed to:

Galas' Exotic Novel Cards
2425 First Avenue, Suite 3-A
San Diego, CA 92101

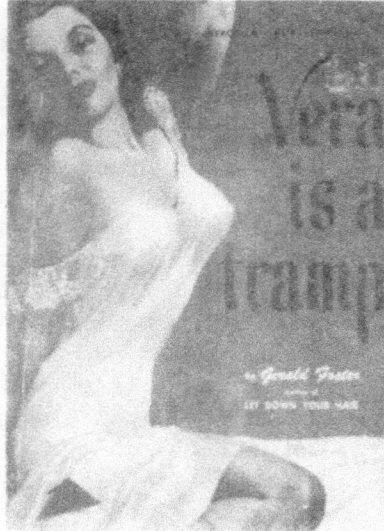

Paperback Postcards
(For Additional Reproductions See Page 55)

Book Review

*A History of Book Publishing in the United States,
Vol. IV, The Great Change, 1940-1980.* by John Tebbel.
Bowker, 1981.

A HISTORY OF BOOK PUBLISHING IN THE UNITED
STATES has been a project of more than ten years'
duration. Volume IV covers the last forty years
of American publishing history. John Tebbel
leaves no doubt that book publishing today
differs dramatically from the so-called golden
age of the 1920s and 1930s, subject of Volume
III. Editorial styles, author advances, pack-
agers and especially the infusion of big money
into publishing through acquisition and merger
are subject to critical notation.
    Of interest to readers of this journal is
the coverage given to mass market paperback publishing. Tebbel rightly puts mass market publishers in different perspectives, depending on
the particular time period with which he deals.
As with other major kinds of book publishing, he
also devotes a section to mass market publishing
in which sketches of major publishers, paperback
and otherwise, are presented. These house bio-
graphies fill in gaps that, although not impor-
tant to understanding the mainstream of modern
publishing, are of great interest to paperback
collectors.
    Besides his own firsthand familiarity with
contemporary publishing, Tebbel's research is
based heavily on the extensive publishing research files of the R. R. Bowker Company. As a
consequence, most of what appears about specific
houses in the mass market section has also been
described elsewhere, sometimes in the pages of
this journal. The genius of Tebbel throughout
his four volumes is his ability to weave a com-

plicated fabric of hundreds of separate publishing houses and thousands of separate publishers into a unified design giving each place
and individual a standing in the march of
American book publishing since 1630. Enter-
taining stories and anecdotes highlight his
comprehensive pattern. --- Thomas Bonn

Book Sellers

The following people sell paperbacks. Many mail out booklists on a regular basis and all are knowledgeable paperback bibliophiles. For specific wants write directly to the addresses below and please include S.A.S.E.

Bill & Pat Lyles
77 High St.
Greenfield, MA 01301
(413) 774-2432

Scott Owen
P.O. Box 343
Moraga, CA 94556

Gravesend Books
Box 235
Poconopines, PA 18350

Anthony Smith
1414 Lynnview Dr.
Houston, TX 77055

PCI
P.O. Box 1308
Hawaiian Gardens, CA 97016

Jeff Meyerson
50 First Place
Brooklyn, N.Y. 11231

Jack Irwin
16 Gloucester Lane
Trenton, N.J. 08618

Fantasy Archives
71 Eight Ave.
New York, N.Y. 10014

Bill Lippincott
Dunbar Hill Rd.
North Anson, ME 04958

Michael Barson
117 Crosby St.
Haverhill, MA 01830

Jan Landau
Rt 2 Box 293
New Castle, Virginia 24127

Family Paperbacks
4016 Central Ave. N.E.
Minneapolis, MN 55412

Sign of the Unicorn Book Shop
604 Kingstown Rd.
Peace Dale, RI 02883

Ed Kalb
3227 E. Enid Ave.
Mesa, Arizona 85204
(602) 830-1855

Jeff Patton
3621 Carolina St., N.W.
Massillon, OH 44646

McClintock Books
P.O. Box 3111
Warren, OH 44485

Fantastic Worlds Bookstore
4816 A Camp Bowie Blvd.
Fort Worth, Texas 76107

Paperback Paradise
468 Centre St.
Jamaica Plain, MA 02130

Barry & Wally Pattengil
Rt 3 Box 508
Waco, Texas 76708

The Old Book Store
210 E. Cuyahoga Falls Ave.
Akron, OH 44310

Murder By The Book
194½ Atwells Ave.
Providence, RI 02903

The Odyssey Shop
1743 S. Union Ave.
Alliance, OH 44601

Larry Rickert
R.D. 1 Box 56C
Augusta, NJ 07822

John Da Prato
61 Puffer Lane
Sudbury, MA 01776

Lone Wolf Mysteries
160 Pennsylvania Ave.
Mt. Vernon, N.Y. 10552

Ralph Kristiansen
P.O. Box 524-Kenmore Station
Boston, MA 02215

Abra-Cadaver
The House of Mystery
110 Dunrovin Lane
Rochester, N.Y. 14618

Remember When Shop
2433 Valwood Pkwy.
Dallas, TX 75234

PD Books
P.O. Box 2132
Pawtucket, RI 02861

Ron Czerwien
7289 W. 173rd Pl.
Tinley Park, IL 60477

Mike Lovinger
2146 Thistlewood
Burton, MI 48509

Keith & Martin Book Shop
310 W. Franklin St.
Chapel Hill, N.C. 27514

Tom Nigra
805 Diane Court
Woodbridge, NJ 07095
(201) 634-7105

Bunker Books
P.O. Box 1638
Spring Valley, CA 92077
(714) 469-3296

Gale Sebert
Sebert's Books
Leivasy, WV 26676

Lucile Coleman
P.O. Box 610813
North Miami, FL 33161

Pandora's Books LTD
Box 86
Neche, ND 58265

Diamond Lake Book Store
1 West Diamond Lake Rd.
Minneapolis, Minn. 55419

Mostly Mysteries Books
398 St. Clair Avenue East
Toronto, Ontario M4T 1P5

The Book Bin
323 Parkdale Center
Waco, Texas 76710
(817) 776-4743

If you are a bookseller and would like your name and address printed in "Book Sellers," please drop us a line. Please tell us if you sell paperbacks by mail and/or have a retail store. If you are interested in selling *Paperback Quarterly*, please write for our wholesale rates.

———————————

Paperback Quarterly is available for retail distribution by bookstores or mail order dealers. An order of ten copies (minimum) costs $15.00 and retails for $29.50 ($2.95 each). All unsold copies are returnable at dealers expense for full refund. Payment must accompany orders except for standing orders which will be billed. Write to *Paperback Quarterly*, 1710 Vincent Street, Brownwood, Texas 76801.

Letters

...I was given a gorgeous, large cover painting for the Lancer Book, THE GHOST DANCERS from 1971. The cover only has a "CM" in the corner. Can anyone help me identify the artist, "CM"?

Sincerely,
Al Grossman
Box 4584
Thousand Oaks, CA
91359

Painting for the Paperback Cover, *The Ghost Dancers*

...To add to Mr. Manesis's list of paperbacks published with dust jackets, I can add the following: Bantam #26 and #462. Also other publishers of paperbacks in dust jacket: Hutchson & Co. (Crime-Book Society series)--British; and Guild Books, also British; as well as Zephyr Books (Stockholm, oversized paperbacks, with plain lettered dust jackets, no photo/art). I'm working on an article on the "Zephyr" line and will send it along as soon as I get it typed.

Truly yours,
Daniel Gobbett

...Robert Bloch sent corrections on the bibliography (which, of course, he had approved earlier in the year):

ATOMS AND EVIL was 1962.
STRANGE EONS is a novel.
COLD CHILLS (1972) was omitted entirely.

All best,
Michael Barson

With regard to the checklist of Gil Brewer paperback books (PQ Winter 1980), I would like to point out some corrections and additions.

To this list should be added SIN FOR ME published by Banner on June 20, 1967 (Banner B50-108). MEMORY OF PASSION was originally published under Brewer's name by Lancer in 1963 (Lancer 70-008). Whether this was later republished by Lancer under the Elaine Evans pseudonym is unknown to me. APPOINTMENT IN CAIRO (It Takes a Thief #3) was copyrighted in 1970 and published on August 3, 1970. WINTERSHADE was published February 1, 1974.

As for A DARK AND DEADLY LOVE, I have to date this as being published on November 2, 1972, and I propose to show why. A DARK AND DEADLY LOVE bears the Lancer book number 447-75403. Lancer 447-75401 (Alice Brennan, TO KILL A WITCH) was published November 2, 1972. Lancer 447-75402 (Grace Corren, EVIL IN THE FAMILY) was published November 2, 1972. Lancer 447-75404 (S. J. Treibich, BURWYCK'S WANDER) was a reissue of an earlier edition (Lancer 73-589). And Lancer 447-75404 (Willo Davis Roberts, SINISTER GARDENS) was published November 2, 1972. It is on this basis that A DARK AND DEADLY LOVE must also have been published on November 2, 1972.

One further point before signing off. In the checklist of STERANKO ART ON PAPERBACKS (PQ Spring 1981) the Berkley Medallion #51944 for WARLOCKS AND WARRIORS should read #S1944.

Sincerely,
Victor A. Berch

...I believe Bill Hamling, who is mentioned in the Bloch interview, founded Greenleaf Classics, which published two of Whittington's titles. It definitely is a porno line, but at least initially they reprinted some in famous, much sought after hardcore erotica.

Sincerely,
James Goodrich

...Regarding my article on Jim Steranko (we are on a first-name basis friendship): Before I submitted the article to PQ, I had Jim edit it so that it would be authentic as to dates, etc. None of the facts were gleaned from anyone but him, so Patton's statement, "I question Hill's research," is unfounded. I still appreciate getting reaction whether correct or incorrect; everyone is entitled to his or her personal opinion.

Yours,
Bunker (M. C. Hill)

William Lyles
77 High St.
Greenfield, MA   01301

Bantam Want List

1   *Life on the Mississippi* by Mark Twain--3rd & 4th printings.
3   *Nevada* by Zane Grey--2nd, 4th, 7th, 8th printings.
7   *The Grapes of Wrath* by John Steinbeck--3rd, 5th, 6th printings.
8   *The Great Gatsby* by F. Scott Fitzgerald--5th printing & copy with Dust Jacket.
17   *Seventeen* by Booth Talkington--4th printing
18   *What Makes Samm Run?* by Budd Schulberg--2nd printing
25   *Bugles in the Afternoon* by Ernest Haycox--3rd & 4th printings
42   *Road to Folly* by Leslie Ford--2nd, 3rd, 5th printings
44   *The Cold Journey* by Grace Zaring Stone--4th, 5th, & copy with Dust Jacket
54   *The Love Letters* by Chris Massie--2nd printing
56   *The Tonto Kid* by Henry Herbert Knibbs--4th printing
60   *The Kennel Murder Case* by S.S. Van Dine--2nd printing
67   *The Bruiser* by Jim Tully--copy with Dust Jacket
73   *The Last of the Plainsmen* by Zane Grey--2nd printing
75   *Cannery Row* by John Steinbeck--3rd, 5th, 9th & copy with Dust Jacket
82   *Ride The Man Down* by Luke Short--3rd printing
83   *Up Front* by Bill Mauldin--5th printing

● ● ● Also need copies that have decorated endpapers for the following Bantam Books: 4, 5, 8-10, 12, 14, 15, 95, 97, 98 -- though I'm not sure these had decorations. ● ● ●

Galas' Exoticards

2425 First Ave., Suite 3-A   ●   San Diego, CA 92101

A set of 8 Full-Color Litho Reproductions of Covers from the 1950s on Giant Postcards: $6 a set/$10 for two sets.

- Vera is a Tramp
- Big City Hellcat
- Bad as the Rest
- Sin Cruise
- Dime a Dance Queen
- Boy Madness
- Slum Doctor
- Sins of an Aspiring Actress

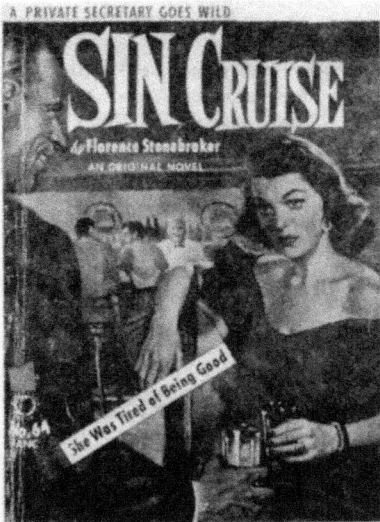

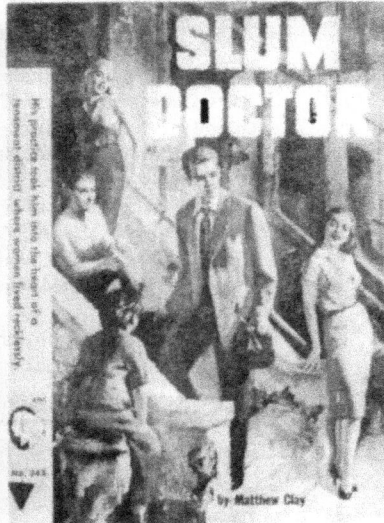

www.ingramcontent.com/pod-product-compliance
Lightning Source LLC
Chambersburg PA
CBHW021226020426
42331CB00003B/478